FLAME STARTER
The Art of Self-Mastery

Elzie D. Flenard III
Foreword by Dr. Larry T. Barnett, THD

Milwaukee, WI

FLAME STARTER: The Art of Self-Mastery

Copyright © 2022 Elzie D. Flenard III

All rights reserved. No part of this book may be reproduced or transmitted in any form or by any means, electronic or mechanical, including photocopying, recording, or by any information storage and retrieval system without the written permission of the author or publisher, except where permitted by law.

ISBN: 979-8-218-09841-4

Library of Congress Control Number: 2022920433

Cover Design & Typesetting: Anita Clinton Enterprises, LLC
Published by: Flenard Enterprises, LLC – Publishing Division

For questions or concerns, visit: www.elzieflenard.com.

DEDICATION

This book is dedicated to every dreamer out there that has a vision. To that mother who wants to realize her full potential. To that dad who had put his dreams on hold and is ready to unleash his greatness. My hope is that through mastering YOU, you will, in turn, spark the flame within you and ignite others around you to do the same.

TABLE OF CONTENTS

FOREWORD i

INTRODUCTION 1

CHAPTER ONE: LET'S TAKE A TRIP DOWN MEMORY LANE… 9

CHAPTER TWO: THE BEST OF THE BEST DO IT… 19

CHAPTER THREE: ARE YOU WILLING TO SHIFT WHEN NEEDED? 29

CHAPTER FOUR: WHAT DID YOU LEARN? 37

CHAPTER FIVE: ARE YOU WILLING TO POUR INTO OTHERS? 42

CHAPTER SIX: YOU MUST SET THE STAGE… 48

CHAPTER SEVEN: YOU ARE ONE OF A KIND… 55

CHAPTER EIGHT: ARE YOU OK WITH YOU? 60

CHAPTER NINE: DON'T LET IT KEEP YOU DOWN… .68

CHAPTER TEN: NO MATTER WHAT, JUST DO IT! 74

CHAPTER ELEVEN: CLOSE YOUR EYES, CAN YOU SEE IT?	78
CHAPTER TWELVE: IT'S YOURS TO CLAIM	85
CHAPTER THIRTEEN: KNOW WHAT SEASON YOU ARE IN	91
CHAPTER FOURTEEN: REMEMBER THE GOLDEN RULE	99
CHAPTER FIFTEEN: THE EMIT PRINCIPLE	109
ACKNOWLEDGMENTS	vi
ABOUT THE AUTHOR	viii

FOREWORD

Feed the flame! I have been extremely blessed to have enjoyed a myriad of experiences that afforded me many opportunities to interact with a variety of people from all levels of society. Teacher, athletic director, basketball coach, principal, collegiate and high school level basketball official, a sports clinician, restaurateur, presenter, speaker, missionary, mentor, pastor, father, husband, and author, to name a few. During life's journey, I experienced ups and downs, failures and successes, setbacks, and comebacks. Although there were times when, intellectually, I didn't know quite how to move forward or how to understand what I was looking at or dealing with, spiritually, there was always something burning on the inside that propelled and changed the trajectory of my life. Fortunately, God always has a "ram in the bush!" Someone who would provide guidance, direction, correction, and grace. My journey would have been greatly facilitated if I could have benefitted from the pearls of wisdom and "Elzisms" presented in *Flame Starter!*

For more than two decades, it has been my distinct pleasure and privilege to serve as a spiritual father and pastor to Elzie Flenard and his family. The natural order of life would suggest that children learn from their parents. Unashamedly, the son has truly taught the father many wonderful lessons in this easy-to-read, inviting, down-to-earth guide on not just being an entrepreneur but on how to succeed at living your best life. The principles of faith, discipline, interpersonal communication, and interaction are presented in a manner that is engaging and encouraging.

FLAME STARTER | FOREWORD

Elzie's passages from childhood to adolescence to adulthood, along with his candid transparency, provide a road map that does not take the shortest path to life's victories but the most enduring and effective road to fulfillment and self-appreciation. The concrete examples and glimpses of his life effectively illustrate that all things truly are possible to those whose purpose is greater than a simple concern for self. The examples of perseverance, determination, will, and a sincere appreciation for others have practical applications for secular as well as spiritual arenas.

Without knowing it many of the *"Elzisms"* on being open to being shaped, zigging and zagging, being irreplaceable to be replaceable, no excuses just execution, getting up more, taking ownership of your journey, and loving them as you love you have been an integral part of my life. Elzie has done a phenomenal job of gathering these valuable proverbs and arranging them in a manner that is both practical and applicable for anyone who has the audacity and faith to dream, plan, and dares to be great. The message of *Flame Starter* reaches across the superficial barriers of political ideologies, age gaps, gender, ethnicity, and religion and points to the possibility of not only dreaming the impossible dream but realizing its manifestation.

If there is a book you need to read in this season of your life that will Educate, Motivate, Inspire, and Transform you from where you are to where you desire to be, it is *Flame Starter*.

After four decades of public service, education, and ministry, I am so grateful to acknowledge that the son has not only blessed the father but has fueled the fire even more.

FLAME STARTER | FOREWORD

In the Old Testament book of Proverbs 27:17, the Word of God says, *"(17) Iron sharpeneth iron; so a man sharpeneth the countenance of his friend."* Allow *Flame Starter* to restore the edge and the flames of your life.

Larry T. Barnett, Sr.BS, MS, ThD
Pastor of St. John Praise & Worship Center Ministries
Author of De-Cloaking The Holy Ghost

INTRODUCTION

Can you remember the first time you saw a rocket launch? *If you've never seen one, take a moment to search and watch it before moving on.*

I was four years old when the *NASA Challenger Mission* launched. There had been other *NASA* missions before, but this one was different. Two years earlier, *NASA* launched the *"Teacher in Space"* project:

> *"Announced by Ronald Reagan in 1984, the pilot program was designed to inspire students, honor teachers, and spur interest in mathematics, science, and*

FLAME STARTER | INTRODUCTION

> *space exploration. These pioneering educators, who would go into space as payload specialists (non-astronaut civilians), would then return to their classrooms and share their experiences with students."*[1]

As a result, Christa McAuliffe was the first teacher selected to go to space. Her inclusion in the mission sparked interest, and on the launch day, children and adults worldwide watched with excitement.

As the countdown reached zero, there was an immediate massive fire shooting out of the bottom of the rocket. I have since learned that the fire was generated through a process called combustion. For combustion to occur, three elements must be present: fuel, oxygen, and heat. After the initial combustion, the rocket began to take off. However, approximately 70 seconds later, another mixture of fuel, oxygen, and heat ignited another combustion.

FLAME STARTER | INTRODUCTION

Houston, we have a problem!

That second combustion was not supposed to happen. A failure of two crucial components of the aircraft allowed hot gas to leak into a tank causing its contents to ignite, destroying the aircraft. As a result, the crew members tragically lost their lives on the mission.

From this incident, I recognized that combustions are powerful and highly impactful when adequately managed. Still, they can also be destructive and tragic when unplanned or improperly handled.

Like combustion, what's inside you is powerful and designed to positively impact the world when properly managed. On the flip side, when improperly handled, the results could lead to un-fulfillment and destruction. If the former is what you desire for your life, then you have the right book. It is uniquely designed to assist you in your journey to becoming, what I call, a *Flame Starter*.

Just as fuel, heat, and oxygen are crucial elements for combustion, three elements must be present for *Flame Starters*: education, motivation, and inspiration. I call it the **EMIT Principle,** and the formula is:

Education x Motivation x Inspiration = Transformation

In order to *EMIT*, the right mix of these three elements is essential because there is a direct correlation to the level of transformation that you can achieve. For example, you may be highly educated but not motivated. Your lack of motivation will impact inspiration, therefore limiting the amount of transformation you have. On the flip side, if you are educated, motivated, and inspired at level 10, your level of transformation will also land at level 10.

THE FLAME STARTER MENTALITY

Being a *Flame Starter* is a mentality, a way of being. For

example, if you remember Kobe Bryant's Mamba mentality. He stated,

> *"the Mamba mentality is a way to live; it's trying to get better every day. It's just the simplest form of trying to get better at whatever you're doing."*[2]

In other words, it is the way that you go about doing things. It doesn't matter if it's basketball, podcasting, career advancement, or business; a certain mentality and approach is necessary. And that's what I'm getting at with *Flame Starter* – it is a mentality about how you go about whatever you do. It doesn't matter what you do; it's more of how you think about it, as you go about it.

Therefore, you ignite your flame when your level of transformation breaks free from your limiting beliefs, and you embrace the law of the universe that energy cannot be created nor destroyed but only change forms.

When I reference flames, there are particular

characteristics:

1. Flames are attractive…
   - They attract other flames *(real recognizes real)*
   - They attract accelerants *(people that help them flame up)*
2. Flames are dangerous…
   - To others that don't understand their intensity
   - To those that are not flames
   - To themselves, if they are not careful
3. Flames are HOT…
   - They inspire others
   - They drive themselves and others

When your flame is ignited, you trans-form into your best possible self and begin living life as a *Flame Starter*.

WHY YOU ARE READING THIS BOOK

This book is written for high-achieving entrepreneurs.

FLAME STARTER | INTRODUCTION

Those who use their creativity, innovation, and talents in their work. It walks you through the core principles I have used along my journey to find my place in the ecosystem.

I call them *Elzisms*, and they provide practical insights you can apply inside your business. They will strategically prepare you for that next opportunity, whether that's transitioning from corporate to entrepreneurship or advancing to the next level in your existing business.

At the book's conclusion, I desire that you feel energized, motivated, inspired, and ready to take on the world. Like the massive amount of fire seen before a rocket launches, the world is desperately waiting to see and experience an enormous amount of fire from you. In other words, we are awaiting your flame to be lit.

Let's get started…

BE AWARE OF FLAME SUCKERS

Flame Suckers are the villains of *Flame Starters*. They are the haters. They look at other flames and always have something to say. They say things like:

- *"Why does he/she do it that way?"*
- *"He or she is too much."*
- *"Are they really who they say they are?"*

They are people who come around just because they want to be close enough to see what you are doing so they can hate on it. They don't have flames of their own, and/or they try to leverage your flame to come up.

Remember this, *Flame Suckers* can only extinguish your flame if you <u>allow it</u>!

CHAPTER ONE:
LET'S TAKE A TRIP DOWN MEMORY LANE...

"You cannot control what happens to you, but you can control your attitude toward what happens to you, and in that, you will be mastering change rather than allowing it to master you."[3]
~Brian Tracy

My mom and dad divorced when I was about five or six. We lived in the city of Chicago in a neighborhood where we couldn't play outside. In one of her many moments of wisdom, my mother decided she did not want to raise her four children as a single mother in the city, so we relocated about six hours away to Mounds, IL. My grandmother had ties to the area. It is where her and her husband raised their five children, and retired.

I don't remember many good things from my first five years of life. However, I do remember witnessing domestic violence and abuse. I remember being confused and thinking, *"Why is he hitting her?"* I knew that my mother was not happy and was hurting. As a result, I learned at an early age how masked pain looked and felt.

Among other things, the relationship with my father taught me the lesson of restoration and redemption. For a large part of my childhood, my father wasn't in my life. There were no happy birthday calls or letters. Nor were there birthday parties or looking into the stands to see him cheering me on. Although there were scars, that experience shaped who I am today. As a result, I "decided" I wanted a family, and was dead set on being the best father and husband I could be. I knew what not to do. How not to be.

ACKNOWLEDGE WHAT HAPPENED

Often, our childhood experiences impact how we show up in the world as adults. You may have had a similar experience or something else that impacted your childhood. Whatever your thing is, you can't ignore what happened. Whether good or bad, you must come to grips with the fact that it happened and that there's nothing you can do to change it. It's not about determining who's to blame, but how you will move forward and grow from what happened.

BE HONEST WITH YOURSELF AND FEEL THE FEELS

We often try taking the position of, *"I don't care; it doesn't affect me!"* That's our pain speaking out loud. When in reality, we care and it affects us. Therefore, it is vital that you acknowledge how you really feel about what happened. Suppressed emotions often seep out and eventually explode on others. One way or another, it's coming out, even if directed at the wrong people. Thus, you want to be self-aware, starting with being honest with yourself. Are you angry, resentful, bitter, afraid, jealous, disgusted, sad, happy, etc.?

If you cannot pinpoint your feelings toward the situation(s), consider using the *Feelings Wheel.* It is a great resource to help adults and children identify and articulate their feelings.

FLAME STARTER | ELZISM ONE

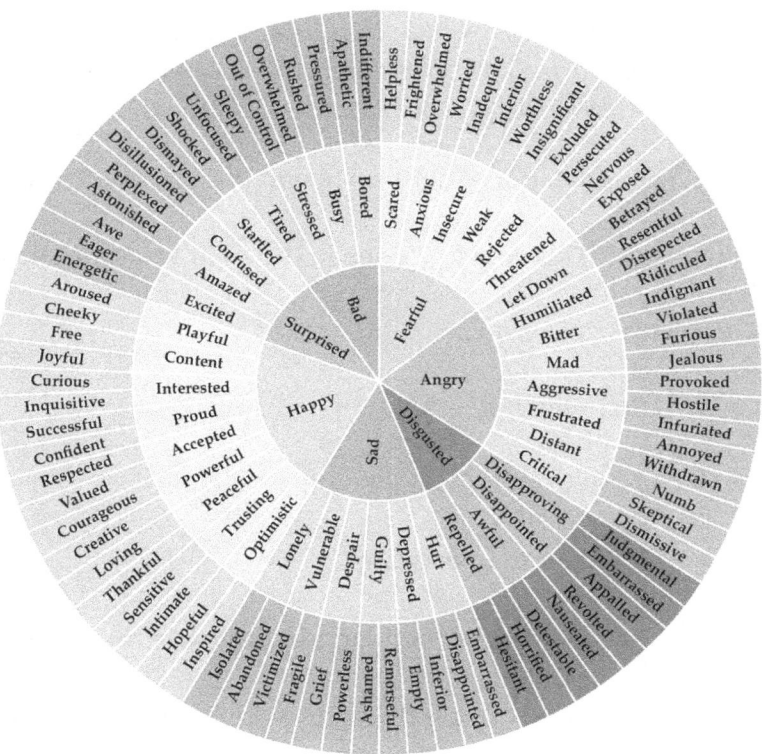

Figure 1: The *Feelings Wheel* is used to help people identify and articulate their feelings.[4]

Once you have acknowledged how you feel – *feel the feels*. An article in *Psychology Today* said,

> *Connecting to ourselves on a feeling level is, for many of us, much easier said than done. Still, with practice, we can learn the language of emotions and become skilled at*

recognizing feelings when they arise, identifying them, experiencing them, and ultimately, honoring them through our communications and actions.[5]

Your feelings matter and it's up to you to acknowledge and honor them. This could be done in different ways and here are a couple to consider:

- Use breathing techniques
- Listen to guided meditation
- Go for a run or exercise
- Share with close confidants or licensed professionals

For me, prayer has worked wonders. Find what works for you and do it.

THE POWER OF EMPATHY, GRACE & FORGIVENESS

Along my journey, I choose to walk in empathy, grace and forgiveness. As humans, we have the power to choose how we respond to the things that happen outside of our control.

There's a saying that reads *"you can't choose what happens in your life, but you can always choose how you respond."*

If I circle back to my dad for a moment, an integral part of my journey was coming to the realization that during my childhood, my father was going through a lot in his life and that our being connected would have likely done more damage than good. God always knows best and has a plan for our lives. In retrospect, I believe this was God's way of teaching me to have empathy and to extend grace to others.

Today I can happily say my relationship with my dad has been restored. God, in his brilliance, was able to take the struggles, pain, brokenness, and restore us back to where we should've been. Now let's be clear, this wasn't easy. It took much prayer, patience, and over time, God restored the relationship.

My dad not only calls to check on me and my family,

but spends time with us as well. My kids don't know the difference. They don't have any of the residue from our past. To them, he's Grandpa. I know, it was nothing but the grace of God that moved us a part and brought us back together when the time was right.

And guess what, God is no respecter of persons. If He did it for me, He's more than capable of doing it for you. Remember, your job is to lead with empathy, grace and forgiveness independent of the outcome.

SEEK SUPPORT IF NEEDED

There are some things that we can work through on our own. However, other things may require professional guidance to help us unpack and work through. Here is where seeking professional support comes in.

I am aware that a public stigma still exists with seeking mental health therapy. Especially in the black community, we don't talk about therapy much; but it's something to strongly consider when dealing with past and current trauma.

As we mentioned earlier, being a *Flame Starter* is about adopting a new mentality, and maybe shifting your view about therapy is part of your adoption process.

* * * * *

My genesis helped me decide early in life that I wanted a family. After witnessing the damage drugs and alcohol had on my family, I promised myself I wouldn't take that path. Instead, I chose to be sober-minded and focused on what's most important: treating women with respect and love, putting family first, and never giving up.

With that, I want to encourage you to work on embracing your genesis, even when it's uncomfortable.

> 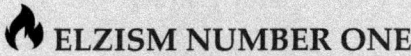 **ELZISM NUMBER ONE**
> Embrace Your Genesis, Even
> When It's Not Comfortable

CHAPTER TWO
THE BEST OF THE BEST DO IT…

"My best skill was that I was coachable. I was a sponge and aggressive to learn."[6] ~Michael Jordan.

My entrepreneur moniker is *The Mayor*. I got the name from marketing coach, Pat Miller, also known as *The Idea Coach*. I hired him to assist us with *Podcast Town's* business strategy and direction. During one of our meetings, he stared off into space for a second *(which is always scary for creatives)* and said,

> "You know what, you're the mayor. The way you show up, the way you preside, the way you handle your business, the way you diplomatically tell the truth, you're the mayor. I'm going to call you The Mayor."

From there, we started testing the name in the market on social media and otherwise, and it stuck and resonated with people. At that time, we knew we were on to something, and even as my personal brand started growing, we began taking that concept to the next level. Today, I'm not the mayor of *Podcast Town*; I'm the mayor of my entire brand.

As I look back on it, I realize that meeting alone was priceless because it changed the trajectory of my brand. Without that marketing coach, my business would be different; and we would not have made the progress we have made thus far.

EMBRACE SELF-AWARENESS

We spoke briefly about self-awareness in *Elzism One*, so let's define it here. According to Jean Graves and Travis Bradberry, the authors of *Emotional Intelligence 2.0*,

> "Simply put, to be self-aware is to know yourself as you really are. Initially, self-awareness can come across as a somewhat ambiguous concept...Awareness of yourself is not just knowing that you are a morning person instead of a night owl. It's deeper than that. Getting to know yourself inside and out is a continuous journey of peeling back the layers of the onion and becoming more and more comfortable with what is in the middle – the true essence of you."[7]

It's essentially being in tune with your emotional state at all times. Now understand that this doesn't automatically happen. You have to be intentional about recognizing and managing your emotions. Tasha Eurich states in her *Harvard Business Review* article,

> Research suggests that when we see ourselves clearly, we are more confident and more creative. We make sounder decisions, build stronger relationships, and communicate

> *more effectively. We're less likely to lie, cheat, and steal. We are better workers who get more promotions. And we're more-effective leaders with more-satisfied employees and more-profitable companies.*[8]

Although it will take work to embrace self-awareness, the return on investment is worth it.

SEEK COACHING, TRAINING, MENTORSHIP, AND CONSULTING

Part of self-awareness is knowing when it's time to be shaped and being open to being shaped. This means being aware of who, what, and why you are. Then knowing why you are looking to improve, enhance or elevate to the next level. At this stage in life, it behooves you to seek guidance from others with the skills, knowledge, expertise and experience you simply don't have yet. This is where coaches, trainers, mentors, and consultants enter into the picture...

Coaches. I had a somewhat frustrating conversation with a young entrepreneur who asked me, *"If I had to give any advice to a younger entrepreneur, what would it be?"* My response was, *"Without a doubt, I would get a coach. I would hire a coach as soon as I knew what business I wanted to be in and all of the other logistics that go with that."*

He immediately came back with a rebuttal and argued with me about the relevance of hiring a coach. In my head, I thought, *see, here you are proving my point.* In my experience, those of us that are very zealous go-getters don't take the time to understand that we all need to be coached. We all have blind spots or areas that we simply can't see, and sometimes we don't even know what we don't know. This is why we need an outside perspective.

Coaches help you define your goals and hold you accountable to achieving those goals. In essence, coaching shortens your success cycle. According to the *Institute of*

Coaching:

> *The benefits of coaching are many; 80% of people who receive coaching report increased self-confidence, and over 70% benefit from improved work performance, relationships, and more effective communication skills. 86% of companies report that they recouped their investment on coaching and more.*[9]

I'm convinced you will never be as good as you can be without having a coach.

Trainers. Although trainers and coaches work well together, trainers cover different elements than coaches do. While a coach helps push, pull, and drive you to perform at your best, a trainer gives you the specific skills that you need to perform at your best. For example, professional basketball player, Giannis Antetokounmpo has both a coach and a trainer. His coach tells him, *"You are 2 for 10 on the free-throw line, but keep shooting; you're in the right spot; keep your head up; you can do this."* His trainer says, *"Right before you* *release, you're hesitating, causing you to miss to the left of the rim. Don't hesitate. Follow through, and flow in one motion."* As in this example, although the coach and trainer work well together, understand that their functions are very different. Therefore, both may be needed.

Mentors. A mentor is someone who is or has been where you want to be. If we circle back to Giannis, he can't call Coach Budenholzer and say, *"Can you tell me what it's like to be a seven-foot basketball player that plays like a guard and takes a pounding every night from players fouling you because you're so strong and fast?"* Coach Budenholzer would not be able to help him with that, but he might call Kareem Abdul-Jabbar and ask him that question. Kareem could share insights on that because he's been there. So your mentor has been or is where you want to be, and they can help guide you from an experiential perspective. With a mentor, you could bypass some, if not all, of the pot holes along your journey.

Consultants. A consultant will evaluate holistically, give recommendations, and help execute and resolve issues. Let's revisit the free-throw example with Giannis. A consultant might come in to evaluate Giannis and say, *"Ok, your current free-throw percentage is 50%. To get it to 70%, you need to work on your upper body strength and hire a trainer to work out the glitch."* The consultant identifies the issue objectively and gives recommendations on what needs to be done. And then, your coach and trainer will help you execute those recommendations.

BE SHAPEABLE

As high-achievers, like the young entrepreneur I mentioned earlier, we think we got it because we know everything and no one can tell us anything. However, most people who have ever accomplished anything in life will tell you that being shapeable or coachable was vital to their success.

Just as I realized I don't know everything, you may have to come to the same conclusion. Along with that, you must also get to the place where you are open to being shaped. There is no benefit in hiring coaches, trainers, mentors, and consultants if you cannot receive constructive feedback and correction.

* * * * *

If I hadn't decided to hire the marketing coach for my business, I would most likely not be the mayor of my brand. In addition, my brand would not be what it is today. So I want to encourage you to work with coaches, trainers, mentors and consultants as needed, and be open to being shaped in the process.

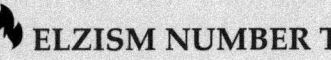 ELZISM NUMBER TWO
Be Open to Being Shaped

<u>CHAPTER THREE</u>

ARE YOU WILLING TO SHIFT WHEN NEEDED?

"The only impossible journey is the one you never begin."[10]
~Tony Robbins

History has many examples of organizations leading in their markets who failed to shift as the environment changed. One example that comes to mind is the story of Blockbuster and Netflix.

In 1985, the first Blockbuster opened, and, within three

years, they had grown to 400 stores. By 1992, they were the undisputed king of movie rentals, with over 2,800 stores domestically and internationally. This exponential growth was in alignment with a major industry shift. In Blockbuster's 1993 SEC *(U.S. Security and Exchange Commission)* filing, they stated:

> *The home video industry has experienced substantial growth since 1980. This growth is largely a result of the increase in the number of videocassette recorders ("VCRs") in use both domestically and internationally. Technological advances have improved the dependability, portability, picture quality and convenience of VCRs. Furthermore, many VCRs are now moderately priced...VCR unit sales in the United States have remained relatively constant during the past five years, averaging approximately 12,000,000 units per year, while VCR market penetration in the United States has grown significantly, increasing from 53.3% in 1987 to 80.5% in 1993.* [11]

Then in the mid-1990s, there was another industry shift. DVDs *(digital video discs)* and DVD players entered the scene, and consumers loved them. DVD player sales increased from 315,136 units in 1997 to 21,994,389 units in 2003.[12] This industry shift opened the door for another movie rental company, Netflix, with its online DVD rental service.

Initially, Netflix struggled to become profitable. Therefore Blockbuster simply ignored them. In fact, Netflix approached Blockbuster twice with a proposal to merge, and Blockbuster laughed them out of the room. At the time, Blockbuster saw Netflix as a little ant in the market. After all, at its peak in the early 2000s, Blockbuster had over 9,000 stores with 84,000 employees worldwide and generated billions in revenue.[13] However, that would soon change.

In the mid-2000s, Netflix began to gain traction, and Blockbuster realized that there was something to online movie rentals and streaming, and they launched an online service. By 2006, Blockbuster had 2 million subscribers,

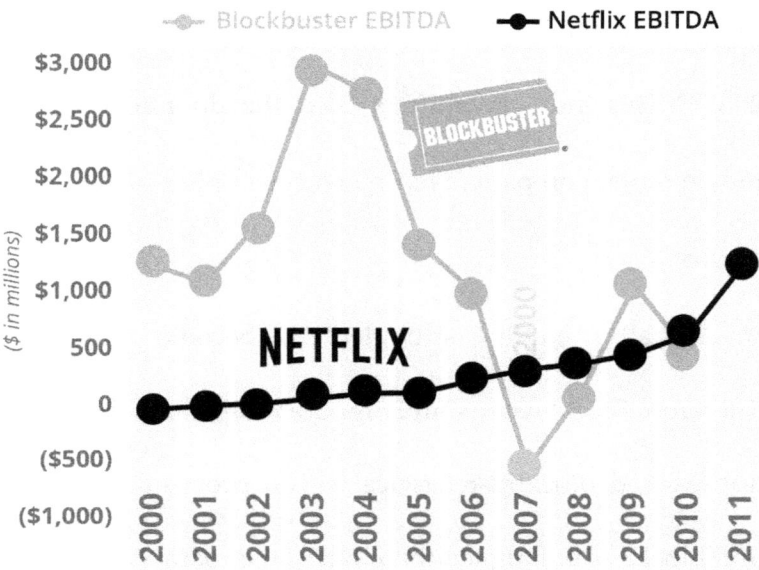

Figure 2: The comparison of Blockbuster vs. Netflix EBITDA (earnings before interest, taxes, depreciation, and amortization) from 2000-2011. Blockbuster filed for bankruptcy on September 23, 2010.[14]

compared to Netflix, with 6.3 million subscribers. Here, although behind the eight ball, Blockbuster still had a chance. However, as franchisees began to complain and launch lawsuits about the online services' negative impact on their business, Blockbuster executives stepped back and didn't put much effort into the online service.

On the flip side, Netflix stayed the course, chomping along like the little engine that could. In 2008, Netflix signed a deal with Starz to stream 1,000 movies on their platform, and then came deals with Sony, Lionsgate, and Disney in 2010. That same year, Blockbuster filed bankruptcy.

STUDY THE ENVIRONMENT/INDUSTRY

Whatever area or field you are in, you want to study your environment/industry. Our world is constantly changing; we see new developments, technology, inventions, and regulations daily.

In our Blockbuster and Netflix story above, Netflix could see and take advantage of the shifts in the movie rental industry. They were listening to the market, watching it, and considering what the market wanted and needed.

Like Netflix, we also listened to the market here at *Podcast Town*. Our market needed an authentic and engaging way to connect with potential and existing customers that provided the ability to develop and grow deep relationships. As opposed to, what is sometimes considered, the surface-level relationships that we make on social media.

We saw that brands could benefit from the reasonably new video and audio podcast relational medium, especially business-to-business. And that's why I believe *Podcast Town* was able to survive amid a global pandemic. There was a great need for organizations and businesses to be able to maintain and deepen those relationships, build trust, grow authority, and increase influence using their voice.

In addition, during the pandemic, the market had shifted, and we couldn't have face-to-face meetings, so the world had to adapt to a virtual environment. For reasons like this, it is imperative that you stay abreast of what's happening in your environment/industry and be willing to adapt to changes. You don't want to become extinct, but be able shift if you want to stay in business.

DOING IT

I once heard someone say, *"You can't just talk about it; you have to be about it!"* You can have the million dollar idea, concept, and plan, and it yields absolutely nothing without action. If you want to see results, you have to do something. I like to call it *zigging and zagging.*

I saw a great illustration on social media that portrayed the difference between the plan we create and reality. The plan was a straight line from point A to point B. However, the reality was a series of lines, with hills and valleys, delays, storms, and obstacle courses to get from point A to point B.

In other words, your journey will most likely not be a

straight path but will require you to zig and zag. There will be hills, valleys, delays, storms, and obstacles, and you will have to adjust. In addition, you must be open to making mistakes and failing because it will happen – a lot.

· · · · ·

Just as Netflix paid attention to the shifts happening in the movie rental industry and acted accordingly, you too must stay abreast of what's happening around you. Then you must be willing to do what no one else is doing. In fact, if you don't get laughed at, you're probably not thinking big enough. Your journey will not be a straight path, therefore it's essential you be willing to zig and zag where necessary.

ELZISM NUMBER THREE
Be Willing to Zig and Zag

CHAPTER FOUR

WHAT DID YOU LEARN?

"Forget what hurt you, but never forget what it taught you."[15]
~Author Unknown

I had a jarring incident that occurred with my *LinkedIn* account. *LinkedIn* is my number one lead generation and social network. Accordingly, I hired a company to assist with lead generation for *Podcast Town* on *LinkedIn*. To make a long story short, some of their actions violated *LinkedIn's* rules, and our account got banned for life. At the time, we had thousands of connections, and I was communicating with potential clients via direct message. It was the method we used to setup and follow-up on meetings with them. As a result of the ban, we lost a lot of business and brand equity. I share this story with you because as you move along your journey, things will happen. Whether it's a success or failure, it's important to take time to examine the WHAT, WHY and HOW...

WHAT. First you want to understand WHAT happened. In my story above, the WHAT was, we were banned for life from *LinkedIn*. Inside of examining what happened, I went through the process we've discussed in the first *Elzism*, starting with identifying the feelings. I was angry, and the majority of the other emotions that extend from the *angry* segment on the *Feelings Wheel. (see page 13)* From there, I had to feel the feels. Afterall, my entire lead generation strategy was greatly impacted by WHAT happened.

WHY. Next is understanding WHY it happened and taking responsibility for your role in the WHY. As the CEO, it's my fault. I should have been more prudent with hiring the company. I should've had an understanding of *LinkedIn's* rules and user agreement. I should have known what the company I hired was doing and monitored the situation more closely. I'm responsible because I should have been closer to what they were doing on our behalf. Had I done my part, the situation probably would not have happened.

HOW

Then you have to determine how you will respond. In my story, I had a choice to make in how I would respond. I could've gone on social media and blasted them by name. I know many people in the business world where I could have said, *"don't do business with this organization because this is what happened."* However, I chose only to put out positive energy and decided I would not share their name with others because I believe that the energy you put out is the energy that comes back. Likewise, you want your response to represent you and what you have created well. Karma has a way of balancing the playing field.

ACT ON IT AND GROW FROM IT

After examining the WHAT, WHY and HOW, it's time for you to take action and grow from the situation. It becomes as an opportunity for you to learn and grow, even if that means restarting.

Again, referring back to the above *Elzisms*, get training and help if needed, and move on in a way you would be proud of. And so that's what I did. I moved on. I took it as an opportunity to refresh and rebrand. I create a new *LinkedIn* account, and today a lot of my content is geared around my personal brand. I still talk about podcasting and other similar topics, but the overarching brand is a little different. In essence, I used what happened as an opportunity to get better, grow, and restart from it.

· · · · ·

As we sum up this chapter, I want to stress that unexpected things will happen along your journey. There's an old saying, *"what doesn't kill you makes you stronger."* Take the incident, determine what happened, why it happened and how you would respond, then act on what you know in a way that represents you well, and grow from it. Above all else, be sure to grab the lesson.

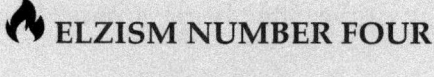

ELZISM NUMBER FOUR
Grab the Lesson

CHAPTER FIVE

ARE YOU WILLING TO POUR INTO OTHERS?

"We make a living by what we get; we make a life by what we give."[16] *~Winston Churchill*

When I look at the journeys and successes of Dr. Phil, Dr. Oz, and Suze Orman, I am convinced that Oprah Winfrey makes people better. You don't leave a role, job, or anything after being around her and not get better, unless you don't want to get better. I don't think that she withholds any knowledge, training, or expertise from people. If you want it, she will give you everything she has, which makes her irreplaceable.

After working with Oprah, people not only become better, they become different manifestations of her business. Meaning, they rise to a level or become so great where they can replace her. Dr. Phil, Dr. Oz, and Suze Orman have gone on to do great things and be a blessing to others in their own unique ways.

In addition, Oprah has transitioned from the Oprah Winfrey show to the Oprah Winfrey Network because she does an excellent job at being irreplaceable by being replaceable. That's why she is who she is.

BECOME A GUIDE FOR OTHERS

Being irreplaceable by being replaceable is taking the first four *Elzisms* and turning them outward. For example, if you are an entrepreneur, manager, supervisor, or leader, you are now using the *Elzisms* to help others get there. You become the guide, helping others embrace their genesis, being open to being shaped, zigging and zagging, and grabbing the lesson. Eventually, they get to the point where they don't need you anymore, which is scary, but it's where you want to be. Here you find yourself at a certain level of uncertainty and discomfort, and one of two things will happen:

1) You'll stay too long and damage your relationships.

2) You'll leave too early and damage your relationships.

So, what ends up happening is you'll have a team that flows so well without you they feel like they don't need you, and that's your indication that you need to either move to a different opportunity/place or there's an opportunity for you to grow in a different role within that team. So you've become replaceable because you're growing and building a team or the people around you to the point where they no longer need you in that capacity. In addition, you're irreplaceable because it takes a lot of maturity, self-awareness, and confidence to give that much to the people around you. So in that way, you become irreplaceable because you're replaceable.

BY DEFAULT, YOU ATTRACT FLAME ACCELERANTS

Flame Accelerants are those individuals who help you flame up. They add to what you're doing, they give to you, and you attract other flames. They may be smaller flames, but they add to the brand or whatever it is. For example, if I had the opportunity to meet Oprah, I wouldn't necessarily ask for anything. For instance, I don't want her to give me a show. I would rather just observe how she treats people because, at the end of the day, that's the thing that stays here when I'm dead and gone.

Money is fine, we need it, and it's great. It's an excellent resource, but when we die, somebody else will spend that money. However, nobody else will have the relationships that you've built. Nobody else will have the memories you created when you treat people the right way. And that's what I mean by flames attracting other flames because real recognizes real. I think that's palpable. I think people can feel that, and they're attracted to that.

There's a quote from author and motivational speaker Leo Buscaglia that speaks well to this:

> *"It's not enough to have lived. We should be determined to live for something. May I suggest that it be creating joy for others, sharing what we have for the betterment of person-kind, bringing hope to the lost and love to the lonely."*[17]

○ ○ ○ ○ ○

In other words, like Oprah our flames should make a

positive impact on the world and those that are connected to us better. So much so, we become irreplaceable by being replaceable.

 ELZISM NUMBER FIVE
Become Irreplaceable by Being Replaceable

CHAPTER SIX
YOU MUST SET THE STAGE…

"We are what we repeatedly do. Excellence, then, is not an act, but a habit."[18] *~Aristotle*

I once heard a consultant share a story that fits perfectly here. She was consulting an organization that had an impactful and influential leader. This leader's personal and private life aligned with the message she taught and encouraged others to apply to their lives. She had been on her journey for years and had achieved a level of influence and success.

However, in an effort to build a solid team to assist her in advancing to the next level, many people had come and gone. A few people were loyal, but they didn't have the knowledge, skill, or expertise to help her progress. In addition, these dedicated individuals played a role in running away those that had the ability she needed. They were just difficult to work with, and their work was subpar.

During the consultation, a conversation about the ability or lack of the current team members to operate in excellence came up. Because these team members had been loyal to her for years, she immediately began to defend them. And then she said, *"Excellence can mean something different for different people. My level or degree of excellence is different from others."*

And the consultant responded, *"Yes, excellence can mean*

something different for people. However, as the leader of your team, you define what excellence means, and your definition becomes the standard for your team. In other words, you are responsible for communicating your level of excellence, and that becomes the base for which they operate."

DEFINE EXCELLENCE FOR YOURSELF

I would like to start this section with the following quote:

> *"Excellence is never an accident; it is the result of high intention, sincere effort, intelligent direction, skillful execution, and the vision to see obstacles as opportunities."*[19] *~Anonymous*

It is the epitome of how I view excellence. You may agree or disagree, but either way, you must define what excellence means to you. If you depend on others to define it for you, you will always be reaching and trying to please other people. That is a recipe for a miserable life experience because you will never be enough to some.

Good old excellence is tricky because when you operate

in it, you will attract other excellent people, ideas, and opportunities. Consequently, the downside of working in excellence, especially when you expect or make excellence the standard for yourself and others, is that it makes people who are not excellent feel uncomfortable. It makes them feel isolated, ostracized, and put on the spot.

I want you to know their feelings are not your fault, and there's nothing you can do about that. You still have to be excellent and understand that in your excellence, in your shining and being who you are, you will offend some people. It will put some people off and cause them to look at you a certain way.

I will never forget when I played basketball, and holding myself to an excellent standard; I wanted to be the fastest I could be. I wanted to make nine out of ten free throws. I wanted to be as excellent of a ball player as I could.

While practicing, one of the guys on my team said to me, *"Hey Elzie, slow down; you're making us look bad."* And I remember thinking, *"All you have to do is speed up, and you won't look bad."* But when you're driven and committed to excellence, sometimes people won't see that as a positive. Despite that, you do you and carry your excellence well.

HOLD YOURSELF AND OTHERS ACCOUNTABLE

As a *Flame Starter*, it's important that you have a vision and mission. Even if you are working as an employee, you should have a vision and a mission that is in alignment with the organization's vision and mission. Either way, it should be personalized for you because you can't grow if you don't have a vision. If you don't know where you're going, how will you get there? Likewise, if you don't have a standard of excellence for yourself that's tangible, then you can't expect others to have a standard.

Once you have defined your standard, I recommend writing it down. It has more power when it's written, and it has to be authentic to who you are, and then you have to share and hold people to it. You have to keep yourself and others accountable to those standards. However, it is also your responsibility to share your standards with others, so that they are fully aware of what you are holding them accountable to. In fact, you want to get their agreement and commitment to those standards. And if they don't agree, you have some decisions to make.

* * * * *

The consultant referenced in the beginning of the chapter wasn't able to shift the client's perspective about what it takes to build a solid team, and the importance of her defining excellence for that team. In the end, they both had a decision to make, and decided not to move forward. At the time of this writing, the organization is still struggling to build a solid team to assist the leader in progressing to the next level.

Operating in excellence sets you apart from the herd. Be sure to make excellence the standard for yourself and others – it truly is a game-changer.

> 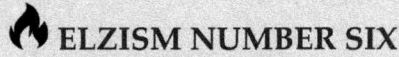 **ELZISM NUMBER SIX**
> Make Excellence the Standard
> for Yourself and Others

CHAPTER SEVEN
YOU ARE ONE OF A KIND...

"Realize that there is only one you that is, was, and ever will be." ~Elzie D. Flenard III

Did you know?

According to the *National Library of Medicine*[20], approximately 300 million sperm are released during the process of conception. Of the 300 million sperm, only about 200 will reach the woman's egg, providing the woman is ovulating. Of the approximate 200 that survived the journey, typically, only 1 will penetrate the egg, which is only viable for 12-24 hours.

WALK IN YOUR GREATNESS

Based on the information above, the chances of you even becoming a human is very, very small. That fact makes you one in 300 million, which is incredibly valuable, rare, and unique. However, at the same time, you're just like every other human, and that point helps keep you balanced. Accordingly, you must realize that there is no greatness that's above your own.

For instance, I was producing a podcast with Dr. Nikia Jordan, who said, *"I appreciate Beyonce. I love what she does. She's great. But I will never elevate someone else's greatness above my own."* And I thought, *Wow!*

When we look at today's celebrity culture, in my opinion, it is the result of people elevating the greatness of others above their own. They clearly see the greatness of others, but they have no idea how great they are because they don't have a good measure of who they are. Their greatness equilibrium is unbalanced.

When I think about things like racism, sexism, ageism, all the isms, and the rich-poor divide, all of those things can, in some ways, be directly tied to an equilibrium imbalance. There are people who are elevating either their own greatness above the greatness of others or others' greatness above their own. Their equilibrium is unbalanced.

Let's look at another example, if we listen to a song that I wrote versus a song that Beyonce wrote. With a balanced equilibrium, people wouldn't look at my song any differently from Beyonce's. They will listen to it if it's a dope song; if it's not, they won't. However, because the equilibrium is not balanced, some people will buy

Beyonce's song just because she wrote it, regardless of whether it's a good song or not. They are respecters of people, and I think if that wasn't the case, everybody would freely operate in their maximum transformation. No one would put others' greatness above their own and we would all be *Flame Starters*. And just think about how different our world would be if everyone walked in their greatness – *oh wee*.

* * * * *

The foundation of this chapter is the dichotomy of the human experience and I really want you to understand it. You are incredibly valuable, rare and unique – 1 in 300 million. You are the only you that ever is, was and will ever be. And, you are like every other human on earth. Not better, not less than, your greatness doesn't compare to theirs and their greatness doesn't compare to yours.

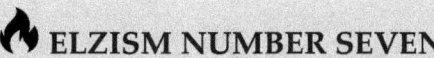 ELZISM NUMBER SEVEN

Understand the Dichotomy
of the Human Experience

CHAPTER EIGHT
ARE YOU OK WITH YOU?

"The truth is: Belonging starts with self-acceptance. Your level of belonging can never be greater than your level of self-acceptance because believing you're enough gives you the courage to be authentic, vulnerable, and imperfect."[21]
~Brene Brown

When I was early in my career, I realized from statistical data research that if I lead with my middle name David Flenard, III on my resume, the chances of me getting a callback go up by 50 percent. And so I consciously chose to leave the very black-sounding name,

Elzie, on my resume. I figured that if potential employers saw Elzie on my resume and didn't call me back, but threw my resume in the trash bin – I didn't want to work for them. Having that mentality saves all of us time, and everybody's happy. Now, I may get fewer callbacks, but the callbacks I do get know, and are ok with the fact that my name is Elzie and I'm black.

BE AUTHENTICALLY YOU

In the 1990s, during Michael Jordan's basketball reign, a Gatorade advertisement labeled, *"Be Like Mike"* spread like wildfire. Not to take anything away from the greatest basketball player of all time, but the advertisement doesn't align with the *Flame Starter* mentality.

At the end of the day, the role of Michael Jordan was already taken. In the *Flame Starter* world, a more fitting label would be, *"Be Like You"*. As we discussed in the last *Elzism*, you are uniquely you, and no one can do you as great as you do you. So just be authentically you. Trust me, more people with be drawn to your authenticity than not.

UNDERSTAND HOW YOU PRESENT, HOW YOU ARE PERCEIVED, AND BE OK WITH IT

I am a fan of Snoop Dogg. He is authentic and OK with who he is and how he presents to other people. He is a product of the streets, smokes weed, and is a smart and successful businessman. We see him in environments and partnerships that don't seem like a good mix. I have even heard him say things like, *"This pairing doesn't make any sense,"* because he realizes how he presents and how he's perceived. He understands it and chooses not to change it because he's OK with the result either way. I believe the thing that made him successful is that he's done all of the *Elzisms* and is OK with who he is.

How you present is all about how you show up in the world. It's your physical appearance, attitude, demeanor, and how you speak, to name a few. Case in point, the way I choose to speak is very intentional. When I open my mouth, you'll know two things:

1. You're talking with an intelligent human who cares about people.
2. If we talk for any length of time, you'll know that I'm about my business and I don't like to waste time.

That's how I present.

In addition to understanding how you present, you want to understand how you are perceived, and the difference between how you want to be perceived versus how you are actually perceived. You may find that the two are not in alignment. All of this really plays off of the self-awareness piece we discussed in *Elzism One*.

For instance, some people might perceive me as a sellout because I don't talk, dress, walk, or show up the way they think I should. Therefore, they might not perceive how I present the way I intend them to, and I have to be ok with that. I think the critical part is understanding and embracing that may be a thing. You must be ok with how you present and how people might receive what you present. Your job is to be intuitive about how people act and respond with their words, and read between the lines of what they're saying and what they're not saying.

Let me give you another example, if I walk into a room as a 5'11" black man, wearing a durag on my head, a sports jersey with my pants sagging, and an entourage, depending on who's in the room, they are going to react a certain way. If I'm in a room with middle-aged white business people, there's going to be a different response than if I walk in the

FLAME STARTER | ELZISM EIGHT

room with people who also have entourages with durags and sagging pants. In the latter environment, I would be most likely welcomed and fit right in; however, in the former environment, security may be called.

So here's the point, how you choose to present, is neither right nor wrong; it's just different. Depending on the environment; the perception may also be different. To understand that perception, you must listen, watch, and take notes. Whatever the outcome, you must accept this is how you're perceived in that environment. And then it's up to you to choose how you move forward.

Along with that, you determine what actions or non-actions you want to happen when you enter an environment. If you observe and don't receive the response you desire, you have the power to change how you present to obtain the desired response.

In addition, there may be times when you want to present a certain way in a particular environment. So you must understand what the environment calls for and what fits within the way you want to present. I think, in large part, it is understanding your audience, how they perceive and receive information, how you present that information, and when there's alignment. And again, depending on the situation, what you are trying to communicate may or may not be ideal.

* * * * *

All of this is only possible when you've done the self-awareness work, you know who you are, and you are comfortable being you.

I have done and continue to do the work, and this is why I'm very comfortable using Elzie on my resume and presenting how I present without being offended when I'm overlooked or people perceive me in a different way. The same is true for you. Remaining cognizant of how you present and how others present to you is vital.

> **ELZISM NUMBER EIGHT**
> Understand How You Present,
> and How Others Present to You

CHAPTER NINE
DON'T LET IT KEEP YOU DOWN...

"There's nothing wrong with getting knocked down, as long as you get right back up."[22] ~Muhammad Ali

Growing up, I was a fan of the *Super Mario Bros.* video game. The game's main characters were Mario, his brother Luigi, and the bad guy Bowser and his minions. The overall goal of the game was to make it through the eight worlds by defeating Bowser and his minions to rescue Princess Toadstool.

Starting off, making it through the first world was a challenge. I would lose and have to start over, lose and start over, lose and start over. I eventually was able to defeat the first world, and go through the same process in the next world – until I finally defeated Bowser in the eighth world. This took about a year of playing the game to rescue the princess.

After the initial rescue, the game allowed me to replay the eight worlds with more complex obstacles and challenges. Although it didn't take a year this time around, it did take some additional time to make it through the eight worlds successfully.

REALIZE THAT YOU ARE GOING TO GET KNOCKED DOWN

I got knocked down a lot in the *Super Mario Bros* game and

had to start over. There were times when I thought I had it, and out of nowhere, a minion would get me. The next time, I knew to look out for that minion, and instead there was another surprise…gotcha. When you learn to look for the left hook, sometimes here comes the right hook.

What I'm trying to say here is, you can't foresee or plan for everything that will come your way on your journey. You will be surprised by the unexpected, and you will be knocked down.

REALIZE THAT OTHERS ARE WATCHING YOU AND ARE INSPIRED BY YOUR PERSEVERANCE

As referenced in the *Introduction*, others are affected by your flame. Some people are warming their hands by your flame. They are watching what you are doing and how you are doing it to get motivated and inspired. They are also taking notes to use for their own journey. Essentially, you become the example that their dream is possible; it can be done.

On the flipside, there will also be those that hate on you. There is nothing you can do to change that. Instead, take the hate from the haters and use it as fuel for your fire. In the natural, when you add fuel to a fire, the flames elevate. If you do have a response, thank them for lighting it up.

THE MORE YOU GET UP, THE STRONGER YOU GET

Strength is created when you know how to manage and move past adversity. In a perfect world, everything would be peaches and cream. There would be no valleys, obstacles, losses, just smooth sailing. Unfortunately, it doesn't work like that – you will get knocked down. And every time you get back up, the stronger you get.

When I think about this *Elzism*, I think about my mom, raising four kids as a single mother. Every Thanksgiving,

Christmas, birthday, back to school shopping, and other times had to be stressful. However, I watched her get up for the battle every single time and continue to do what she needed to do to provide for us. Because of this, I did my best not to be a burden for her and to make her proud. It also entrenched in me this attitude of never giving up, never throwing in the towel, or never saying it's over. If you have another breath in your body, it's another opportunity to go at it again. My mom is one of my biggest inspirations.

* * * * *

When I was playing *Super Mario Bros.*, each time I got knocked down, I got back up smarter and more determined to win. The power was in the getting up. You too will find your strength in the getting up, so be sure to get up more!

ELZISM NUMBER NINE
Get Up More

CHAPTER TEN

NO MATTER WHAT, JUST DO IT!

"Great things come from hard work and perseverance. No excuses."[23] ~Kobe Bryant

In high school I had this mentality of no excuses, just execution. On the basketball court, whenever we would run a play, if the passer didn't throw a good pass, there was no excuse. Instead, I figured out a way to get the ball. It was my responsibility to make it happen, even if it meant I had to take an extra step or extend my arms further. I was willing to do whatever I had to because there were no excuses.

HOW TO OVERCOME EXCUSES

It is so easy to make excuses for why we couldn't or didn't do something in today's environment. We can use racism, sexism, ageism, or whatever other ism as an excuse. We can use family, school, etc., as the reason it didn't happen. And just to be clear, all of those may be legitimate, but that doesn't mean you use them as crutches or reasons you can't progress.

Sometimes we tend to make things more complex than they really are. Some things are just cut and dry, and this concept happens to be one of those things. We all figure out how to do what we want to do, period! We find ways to take that vacation, to get those new Jordans or that designer purse. If it's something we want, our creativity kicks in. Therefore, this *Elzism* works the same, get creative and find a way to get it done. In her book, *"Everything is Figureoutable,"* Marie Forleo said it this way,

> "If it's important enough, I'll make the time. If not, I'll make an excuse."[24]

You will face challenges and obstacles along the way, but there is no excuse. At the end of the day, you have to execute.

· · · · ·

Just as I did when I was playing basketball in my youth, no matter what or how it comes your way, you must do whatever you have to do make it happen. There are no excuses, just execution.

ELZISM NUMBER TEN
No Excuses, Just Execution

CHAPTER ELEVEN

CLOSE YOUR EYES, CAN YOU SEE IT?

"I used to imagine what it would be like to do what Jim Brown was doing. I used to imagine what it would be like to be like a Tony Dorsett. I used to imagine what it would be like to be like a Walter Payton. I was imagining Emmitt Smith doing exactly what they were doing."[25] ~Emmitt Smith

Every Saturday morning as a kid, there was one television show that I had to watch, *X-men*. As an adult, Marvel created the X-men Film Series. In one of the films, there is a scene with the mutant, Magneto, walking inside a cave. He gets to a part of the cave, and the walking path ends, but there's no bridge for him to cross over. However, this doesn't phase Magneto; he pauses briefly to gain perspective and then he just kept walking. As he stepped off the edge, these metal plates began to line up under his feet. They built step-by-step until he was safely on the other side. He understood the fact that the bridge was not there. He just didn't care. He was confident in his super power and knew that he could command the nearby metal to complete his path.

What's your super power? What can you command to bridge the gap from where you are to where your vision can take you?

Understand, this scene lasted all of five seconds, but in that short moment, I was immediately reminded of my faith. The vision for my life is so big that I will never have all the pieces of the puzzle. Therefore, if I was to wait for all of the pieces, I would never have gotten started. At some point, I had to move out on faith, and just like the plates aligned for Magneto, they began to align for me as well. That looked like opportunities, resources, and favor, as well as the right people crossing my path.

WRITE THE VISION AND MAKE A PLAN.

"Write the vision And make it plain on tablets, That he may run who reads it."[26]

I apply this scripture anytime I'm preparing to go to the next level. Now, as much as I want to be the guy who says, *"I always seek the Lord for direction,"* sometimes I just do things because I want to. However, I do try to pray about everything that I do. Whether personal or business, I ask God to reveal the right way to do it. And then, from there, I visualize it. I literally see myself doing it.

For example, when we opened a second location for

Podcast Town. Before we even went and looked at anything, I closed my eyes and saw the space. I wanted a space that was conducive to live podcast recording. I wanted a control room where the producer could sit and do production. And then I wanted a space where we could have workshops and training.

I saw myself pulling up, getting out of the car, and walking into the space. It was almost like I was there. And then, when I reached out to the broker to look at spaces, she took me to a space five minutes away, and it was what I visualized. Even as we purchased furniture and planed for the ribbon cutting, etc. I saw the sign and the people coming in. I visualized it all, and I lived in that visualization, so much so that when it happened, it wasn't the first time it happened, even though it was the first time it happened.

BE OPEN TO IT HAPPENING DIFFERENTLY THAN YOU THOUGHT IT WOULD HAPPEN

You often think things are going to happen a certain way, but it happens a lot differently than you thought it would. And that's ok. You must remain open and willing to accept what the journey gives you. Because the journey, in many ways, has a life of its own. Even though it's your journey, you are just a part of the journey. And if you're flexible and persistent, the journey will lead you to your destination.

DREAM BIG AND ACT BIG

Over the years, I've been guilty of dreaming big, but the vision is so big that I sometimes act small. And sometimes, my vision and my actions aren't in alignment. In those instances, just like Magneto, I have to believe and take the first step. With big dreams, you're not going to know all the steps, even though you may want to. If you know all the steps to accomplish your vision, it isn't big enough.

This will require you to get out of your comfort zone because magic happens in the uncomfortable zone. Not to mention, the more time you spend in the uncomfortable zone, the larger your comfort zone becomes. It's magic, I tell you.

· · · · ·

With that, I encourage to create your personal vision commercial, close your eyes and watch it often. You can also create a vision board with words and pictures to view on a consistent basis. Either way, it helps to imagine your journey. Ask yourself, if there were no boundaries and money, time or ability wasn't an issue, what would you do? Do that. Do it well. Do it with everything in your soul and watch lives get impacted beyond your wildest dreams.

ELZISM NUMBER ELEVEN
Imagine Your Journey

CHAPTER TWELVE
IT'S YOURS TO CLAIM

"Sometimes it's the journey that teaches you a lot about your destination."[27] ~Drake

I'll never forget living on the campus at *Southern Illinois University (SIU) Carbondale* and really evaluating the bed I had made. Having graduated with an associates degree in electronics from a local trade school and in between jobs, I felt stuck in a place of indecision and frustration because everyone else around me seemed to be making progress. My sister, her husband and my wife were all in college earning their Bachelor's degrees at *SIU* and on the path to success in their careers. But there I was...stuck. It's funny looking back on it now, but I believe they all got together and conspired to convince me to go back to school and get my Bachelor's degree. Their plan, I believe, was to get me into the college life environment so I could see, hear, smell, envision what it would be like.

So there I was, at an *SIU* basketball game and the atmosphere was electric, the smell of popcorn and youthful excitement permeated the air. I watched the home team squeak out a victory and I remember thinking, *"If this is what the energy is like 'being' a student, I want that."*

I watched my sister, her husband and my wife go to class, study for tests and grind through the college experience and started to crave that *"grind."* I like the grind.

It builds character and helps mold you. The grind creates the spark. It creates the *Flame Starter*. So, I enrolled and graduated with a degree in Electronic Systems Technologies.

As I age gracefully, I've been thinking more and more about self-mastery. You know, being the best possible version of me. This is a process that you never completely master because you are always restarting the process. I like to think about it as levels in life, once you reach one level, the new goal becomes reaching the next one. It is a journey of becoming that doesn't end until you leave the earth.

Today, I realize the things that motivate me, my vision, and my goals are not the same as they were when I was in my 30s. And so it's a constant process of realignment and adjustments. At 40, different things are important to me. That's why I must continue the journey of self-mastery. It directly impacts my business, relationships, manhood, and life. It all comes into greater focus the more you understand yourself and the season you're in.

YOUR LIFE IS...

Your current life is the sum total of the decisions that you have made thus far. Let me say that again,

> *"Your life is the sum total of the decisions that **you** have made."*

That is not an original quote, and I do not know who said it, but I live by that thing. My life is the sum total of the decisions that I've made. Essentially, you make your bed. If you like what your bed gives you, you can keep going. If you don't like it, make different decisions and take different actions.

DECIDE AND COMMIT

Every day I wake up and say to myself, *"I don't like my dad body; I have to change what I'm doing."* I can't eat Red Robin every week and expect not to have a dad body. I have to decide and commit.

You know, when I ask people on my show, *"How did you come to the realization that you wanted to have a different life?"* Over and over again, they say, *"I decided, and I committed to the process."*

Once you embrace this fact, you become powerful beyond measure because now you've taken the power out of the things that happen to you. And you transfer that to everything that happens for you. Author Byron Katie says it like this,

> *"Life is simple. Everything happens for you, not to you. Everything happens at exactly the right moment, neither too soon nor too late. You don't have to like it...It's just easier if you do."*[28]

One of the pivotal moments in my life was when I was in college, and I realized that I could shape my journey; I concluded that I could decide what my life would be like.

And so, I did from that moment on; my life took on a trajectory that allowed me to do things I could not have imagined.

* * * * *

Now understand that this may be easier said than done, and it is a perfect situation to hire a coach, trainer, mentor, or consultant to assist you. Revisit *Elzism Two* for more on the relevance of working with these professionals.

Please understand that this is your journey, and you must take ownership of it.

 ELZISM NUMBER TWELVE
Take Ownership of Your Journey

CHAPTER THIRTEEN
KNOW WHAT SEASON YOU ARE IN...

Just for today, allow yourself to embrace all that you are every moment. Know that you are a vessel of light. Allow yourself to release all doubts about your ability, the mistakes of the past, and the fear of the future.[29] ~Iyanla Vanzant

I was sitting under my gazebo the other day, and I looked at my wife, my daughter, my son, and my life, and I realized that I have enough. Not only do I have enough, but I am also enough. At that moment, I concluded that this current moment is all we have. We don't have the next moment, and the last moment is already gone. Therefore, we can't live in the previous moment, and you can't live in the moment that's to come. You have to embrace the current moment, which allows you to be present in the moment, appreciating and enjoying it. Experience the moment with gratitude, graciousness, and everything in your being to be open, centered, and focused. This is a highly profound place to BE.

MAKE THE MOST IMPORTANT THING THE MOST IMPORTANT THING

The older I get, my kids are getting older too. I realize they're like real human beings, and the time is going so fast. And so just embracing the moment speaks to understanding and prioritizing what's important.

Now it's essential to understand that this doesn't just

happen, and it's easier said than done. You must be intentional about setting boundaries, communicating, enforcing, and reinforcing those boundaries. Therefore, you must take the time to prioritize and make the most important thing first.

Not to brag, but I'm very intentional about my schedule and where and how my family is positioned in that schedule. What do I mean? Although I'm an entrepreneur, I don't have 10-18 hour days. I have business hours, and once business hours are over, I have family time. Now, of course, this doesn't fit tightly in a perfect bun, but it is the guideline I do my best to enforce.

However, I've had clients reach out to me occasionally outside of business hours. And I've had that conversation where I explain my business hours are from this time to that time, because I know I must protect my time. It's the one thing I can't get back.

That said, my clients can't call me on Sunday because I don't work on Sundays, period. Just to reiterate here, it is essential that you are intentional about setting boundaries, communicating, and enforcing those boundaries. The communication piece is critical because if you don't tell people what your boundaries are, they don't know. And you can't hold them accountable because you haven't communicated your boundaries.

Then, the next thing is enforcing those boundaries. For example, you may tell clients, *"My office hours are from 9am-5pm,"* but you work until 8pm. In this instance, you've created and communicated the boundary, but you are not enforcing it. Now I understand that early on in business, it's more difficult because it can take 16 hours a day to learn and grow your business.

But I've resolved that there are many things I could do business-wise that I don't do. And I choose to work 8-hour-ish days. I realize it might take me longer to get to a certain point. For example, if I were to fly to Atlanta every weekend to do my podcast interviews with the movers and shakers there, my podcast would grow exponentially. There's no doubt about it – that's a fact.

However, I don't do that because my priority is to take my son fishing on Saturday. My priority is to attend my daughter's dance competitions. That's my priority. It might take my show longer to get where I want it to go, but that's the sacrifice I'm willing to make to maintain those relationships with my family and give myself space to live in the moment with them. So there is a trade-off, but I think you must be aware of the trade-off and the fruit of your decisions and actions.

NEW SEASONS BRING NEW EXPECTATIONS

Depending on your situation and what you have going on, there will be times when you have to make adjustments. For instance, I enjoy listening to Dave Ramsey and his team. I was listening to the Dr. John Delony show, and he was talking about seasons. He had written a new book, and Dave Ramsey scheduled an extensive marketing campaign to promote the book. And he spoke of having a conversation with his wife and his kids about the adjustments they would have to make for that particular season during the launch of that book. He explained that he wouldn't be as available as he usually is.

So as a family, they talked about it and collectively decided what this season would look like with this temporary schedule. He was adamant about ensuring they understood that this would be just for a season and not for the rest of their lives. After this short season, things would get back to normal, and for the kids, they agreed to travel to Disney World after the tour. With that, the kids had something to look forward to at the end of this season of not seeing their dad every night.

Like Dr. Delony, there will be seasons in your life where you have to make adjustments. However, if you have a family, you have to consider the impact of the adjustment on them. This could work well as long as there are open lines of communication and everybody's on the same page *(including the kids, if applicable)*. And everyone should understand this is only for a season.

I say this because you should remember that anything that needs to grow needs to be watered. If you think about flowers, they need to be tended to in order to grow and blossom. They just do. So, in your seasonal planning, be considerate and understand that this is delicate and that you must pay attention to what's happening in the family unit.

If you're in the season of life where you don't have kids or a spouse, spending 20 hours a day working could be ok for that season, but only for that season because it's not sustainable.

* * * * *

As we close this out, remember what's important, because anything that needs to grow must be watered. Always take the time to embrace the moment.

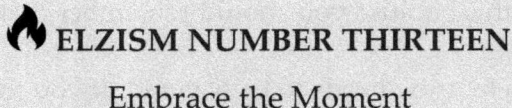

ELZISM NUMBER THIRTEEN
Embrace the Moment

CHAPTER FOURTEEN
REMEMBER THE GOLDEN RULE...

"A new commandment I give to you, that you love one another: just as I have loved you, you also are to love one another."[30]
~John 13:34-35 (ESV)

When we take a broad look at our world, there's so much unnecessary hatred, rudeness, discord, and strife. In many instances, people are expected to pick sides. Even agreeing to disagree can create issues.

A perfect example of this is the LGBTQIA+ community.

FLAME STARTER | ELZISM FOURTEEN

I question why is there so much controversy? Whether you agree or disagree with their beliefs, it can be problematic. If you agree, it becomes an issue with those who disagree and vice versa. With both sides, you end up either right or wrong and not in a place of respect at the human level.

I pose the question, what if there was another option? What if we decided to lead with love and leave space to agree to disagree, and do it in a productive way? In a way that's empathetic, in a way that, at a minimum, causes people to consider a different way of thinking.

Not that we're trying to convince either side of anything, but we're presenting a different opinion. A different perspective. And that being accepted in a way where we can agree to disagree. It doesn't mean we hate each other, but we simply can agree to disagree. We choose to walk in love and respect each other's opinions. This is not easy. If it were, everyone would do it, at least I hope they would. It takes courage, prayer and reflection to get to the place where you understand that taking a position will cause backlash and that you may lose friends or business opportunities as a result. Be brave, be courageous. Embrace the fruit of the decisions you make. It's YOUR bed. Make it well!

Let's look at a business example, Black Girls Code (BGC) is a non-profit organization founded in 2011 by Kimberly Bryant, with the mission:

> *"To increase the number of women of color in the digital technology space by introducing girls 7-17 to computer science."*[31]

The organization's board fired the founder in a hostile takeover due to claims of *"Bryant's misgendering a staff member and creating a toxic work environment."*[32] According to the former employees, *"staff churn was largely attributed to*

Bryant's leadership style, which they describe was 'rooted in fear.' When Bryant was there, they say she would publicly berate managers within meetings, repeatedly calling folks incompetent and urging a manager to 'go back to school' when they were unable to deliver on a certain task."[32]

This, unfortunately is the story of a woman who lit her flame to change the trajectory of young black girls, and she has now been ousted out of the very organization she built. Now, I don't know if the allegations are true or not and I don't know Kimberly personally, but that's not the point. The point is, there is always at least three perspectives in any situation, yours, theirs and the complete truth. Had everyone involved in the *Black Girls Code* situation led with compassion, empathy and understanding, there is little doubt in my mind the situation gets resolved in a way that is better suited for the young black girls the company was built to help.

Some CEOs think that their employees work for them. I happen to think that's backward. As the CEO, you work for them. There has to be mutual respect, because they are your teammates, helping you achieve your vision. In the book, *"Lead Like Jesus,"* the authors stated it this way:

> *"Jesus modeled this perfectly in John 13-14; 'You call me Teacher and Lord, and rightly so, for that is what I am. Now that I, your Lord and Teacher, have washed your feet, you also should wash one another's feet.' Jesus created a community by empowering His followers to serve and then trusting them to do exactly that."*[33]

> *"Leading like Jesus requires leaders to be shepherds and servants, who value each person as an integral part of the organization. These leaders adopt as their core values the principles and practices of Jesus and incorporate those in the organization's training, policies, and systems. When a challenge comes, leaders examine their self-leadership before investigating possible organizational weaknesses."*[34]

Like many things, I think Jesus got it right and we've gotten it wrong. Your staff are not your underlings, they're helping you elevate, so you should treat them as such.

LEAD WITH LOVE, SERVICE, AND JOY

So this is a tough one because, again, it's one of those things where the assumption is that you love yourself. This is why we did the work previously on self-awareness, dealing with your stuff, embracing the journey, etc. All of that leads you to the place of self-love. And when you love yourself, you're not going to disrespect yourself or do things that harm you or others.

Once you've done all the work, the premise is that you lead with love, joy, and service. You come from a place of, *how can you help people?* As opposed to *what they can give me or what can I get?* I've found that planting seeds of love, service and joy, without expecting anything in return, has paid huge dividends for me in my life and business.

You know, when I reach out to people, whether on

LinkedIn or at a networking meeting, I'm literally reaching out to see how I can add value. *How can I help?* If I get business as a result, awesome. If not, then that's awesome as well. So I'm intentional about leading with love, service and joy, and treating people as I want them to treat me. Whether they're the CEO of a Fortune 100 company or a worker at Starbucks, I treat them the same, leading with love, service, and joy.

LOVE IS...

When I think of this concept, I believe one of the world's challenges is that people misunderstand love. As a society, we've tried to redefine it, but the ultimate definition of love is:

> *Love is patient and kind. Love is not jealous or boastful or proud or rude. It does not demand its own way. It is not irritable, and it keeps no record of being wronged. It does not rejoice about injustice but rejoices whenever the truth wins out. Love never gives up, never loses faith, is*

> *always hopeful, and endures through every circumstance...Three things will last forever—faith, hope, and love—and the greatest of these is love.*[35]

Love is all of that, and corrects and chastens. Meaning if I love you and I see you going in the wrong direction, I'm going to tell you, you're going in the wrong direction. However, as I mentioned earlier, we've eliminated that from our society because we cannot disagree. So I think we need to understand that part of loving others is having a heart to correct in love. Not with hate, and not from a place of self-righteousness, but love.

LOVE PEOPLE LIKE GOD LOVES YOU

Now, let's keep it real; I'm not naïve; loving people like God loves you is not easy. Some people can be difficult. They do and say things that sometimes make you want to step out of character.

I won't give specific examples here, but there have been

times when people have done things *for* me, and I could have put them on blast, but I didn't. I could've brought the receipts and destroyed them, but I didn't. And I'm so glad I didn't because usually what ends up happening is the results of the seeds they planted come back to them. I'm clear that I don't have to be the one to do anything harmful to others, but continue to lead with love, service, and joy. That, too, comes back to me.

With that, you have to be disciplined and remember that God gave you a chance. And then another chance. And then seven more chances. And then seven more chances after that. When you love people as God loves you, this means showing people grace after grace.

· · · · ·

So whether it's the LGBTQIA+ community, your co-workers/subordinates, your staff, your waiter/waitress, etc.

be careful of the seeds you plant because those seeds will grow and ripen. If you grow love, love grows. Remember that as a *Flame Starter*, you are the example God calls us to be. So choose to love them as you love you.

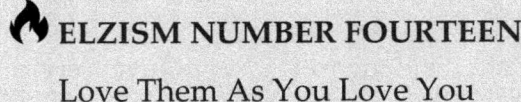

ELZISM NUMBER FOURTEEN
Love Them As You Love You

CHAPTER FIFTEEN
THE EMIT PRINCIPLE

"Self-enrichment is that act of creating a thousand micro wins so that you can have one macro win."[36] ~Lisa Nichols

The *EMIT Principle* is the foundation of the *Flame Starter* mentality. The formula is as such:

Education x Motivation x Inspiration = Transformation

Your level of transformation is in direct correlation with your level of education, motivation, and inspiration. Those levels are determined by you. You are what you say you are and you will do what you say you will do. If you do the work, and put the *EMIT Principle* into practice, you will achieve a peak level of transformation. And this changes as you grow wiser, as you grow older, as you have more experiences, you glean more, and you understand more. Essentially, your level of transformation will become more efficient on the curve as you grow.

So don't be disappointed or discouraged if your level of transformation is not where you want it. These concepts are not easy. If they were easy, everyone would do them. However, things change when you commit to doing the self-work and applying the principles as outlined:

Elzism One: Embrace Your Genesis, Even When It's Not Comfortable. For many people, some sort of trauma has happened in their lifetime. If you are one of them, it's up to you to ensure you deal with it. You can't just smother it and pretend like it didn't happen. Get help if needed, but deal with it because it will negatively impact your flame.

Elzism Two: Be Open to Being Shaped. Most people who have accomplished anything in life, worked with coaches, trainers, mentors, and/or consultants. Not only have they worked with them, but they allowed them to critique and correct them where needed. You must do the same, especially if you want to shorten your success cycle.

Elzism Three: Be Willing to Zig and Zag. Your journey will not be a straight line from point A to point B. There will be a lot of zigging and zagging. Be open and patient with the journey because it will take you to your destination.

Elzism Four: Grab the Lesson. There will be unexpected occurrences on your journey. Be sure to take the time to determine the What, Why, and How, then act in a way that represents you well. You will have scars, but make sure you grab the lesson.

Elzism Five: Be Irreplaceable by Being Replaceable. Work yourself out of the position you're in. Train your team as if you are training them to replace you. Give them everything they need to do so. Hold nothing back. Actively seek to replace yourself. By operating that way, you make yourself irreplaceable. When you give the most, are the chief servant, teach the most, encourage the most, help others the most, you become irreplaceable. You are irreplaceable because most people are afraid to replace themselves. They get comfortable and people love comfort. You will constantly be in an uncomfortable state.

Elzism Six: Make Excellence the Standard for Yourself and Others. Whatever you are doing, excellence should be the only option for you and others connected to you. It not only raises the bar, but it sets you apart from the masses who are not operating in excellence.

Elzism Seven: Understand the Dichotomy of the Human Experience. You are 1 in 300 million, and that makes you rare, unique, and one of a kind. It also makes you just like every other human in the world. Unlike what society believes, it is important that you know there is a level playing ground. No one's greatness is above yours, period!

Elzism Eight: Understand How You Present, and How Others Perceive What You Present. It is 100% your responsibility to know how you show up in the world, and how others perceive you. Once you know, you can decide if you are OK with that, or if you want to adjust it. You determine how you want to be perceived by how you present.

Elzism Nine: Get Up More. You will be knocked down, and sometimes the hit will be brutal. No matter what, you must get back up every time. Your strength is found in the get up...

Elzism Ten: No Excuses, Just Execution. Excuses are dream killers. Don't allow them to hinder, halt, or slow down your progress. Allow your creativity to kick in and keep it moving.

Elzism Eleven: Imagine the Journey. Create your own internal commercial that plays repeatedly in your mind. Visualize where you are going, how you will get there, and rejoice when it happens in the natural.

Elzism Twelve: Take Ownership of Journey. Recognize that your decisions and actions shape the life you either enjoy, regret, or dislike. If you don't like what you are seeing and experiencing, you have the power to change it. It's your journey...claim it!

Elzism Thirteen: Embrace the Moment. The current

moment is all you have. You don't have the next moment and the last moment is already gone. Remember to embrace the present moment, appreciating and enjoying it.

Elzism Fourteen: Love Them As You Love You. Once you've done your self-work, the next step is your outer-work. Meaning, how you interact and treat others. You want to get to the point where you are able to love others as you love yourself.

When the *Elzisms* become your way of life, you achieve peak performance and, therefore, peak transformation. Here, you have broken free from your limiting beliefs, and have embraced the universe's law that energy cannot be created or destroyed, but only changes forms. And so you transform into your best possible self and began living life as a *Flame Starter*...As discussed in the beginning, remember this about flames:

1. Flames are attractive…

    - They attract other flames *(real recognizes real)*.

    - They attract accelerants *(people that help them flame up)*.

2. Flames are dangerous…

    - To others that don't understand their intensity.

    - To those that are not flames.

    - To themselves, if they are not careful.

3. Flames are HOT…

    - They inspire others.

    - They drive themselves and others.

CAUTION…WARNING

When you become a *Flame Starter*, there are some dangers that you must be aware of and adjust accordingly when they appear. As a *Flame Starter*, your intensity can be dangerous to yourself. *Flame Starters* are drivers. We like to get things done. We're Excellent! Sometimes this will hurt us.

Let me give you an example: my body is being affected by *Graves' disease*, an immune system disorder. I'm pretty sure it is the direct result of the stresses that come along with entrepreneurship. There was an extended period of time when I felt really drained and sick. I was literally having to drag myself out of bed and wondering what was wrong with me. I ended up going to the doctor, taking tests and finding out that I'm battling with *Graves' disease*.

On some level, I am glad I know the battle I need to fight, but on another level I question if I could have avoided it somehow. Then, I remember that I have to listen to my own advice and embrace the bed I have made. I must understand that this has happened for me and that God can use this experience to help others.

So as you move forward, I want to encourage you to pay attention to your body and take care of yourself. Your flame is no good if it's not shining as brightly as possible.

Next, we talked about this in the beginning, and I want to reiterate it. As a *Flame Starter*, there will be *Flame Suckers* or haters. These are individuals that look at other flames and always have something to say. They hate because they don't have flames of their own yet because they haven't done the work to *EMIT*. Therefore, they will try to leverage your flame to come up. If you are not careful, they can douse your flame or cause you to slow down your transformation if you spend too much time worried about them. Instead, you focus on *EMITing* and let them be.

EXAMPLE FLAME STARTERS

I didn't want to end our time together on a sour note, so below are some *Flame Starters* you may know. Now understand, I'm sharing their stories so you can see what's really possible. I intentionally picked them because they started with nothing but a vision, determination and grit. They each have done the work, and are reaping the benefits…enjoy!

🔥 MICHAEL JORDAN[37]

Michael Jordan is arguably the best basketball player of all time, but he definitely didn't start out that way. As a child, he loved sports but failed to make the basketball team his sophomore year. At this point, I would venture to say he started working the *Elzisms*.

He made up his mind that he would do whatever he needed to do to make the team the following year. Not only did he make the team, but was recruited by the one and only, Dean Smith, coach at the *University of North Carolina*.

At college, Jordan earned honors and accolades every year until he was drafted by the *Chicago Bulls*. He was the *NBA's Rookie of the Year* and made the *All-Star Team* his first season. Although he faced many obstacles and setbacks along his journey, he lit his flame and positively impacted millions.

🔥 OPRAH WINFREY[38]

Against all odds, Oprah Winfrey became the most notable television show host in the world. As a young child, her parents abandoned her, leaving her to live with her maternal grandmother, on the farm where she would entertain the animals.

At the age of six, she moved back with her mother and siblings in a low-income neighborhood. Life with mom was difficult, even to the point of experiencing sexual abuse. She also spent time with her father, who emphasized the importance of education.

Oprah would begin speaking and taking other opportunities to be on stage in front of an audience. She loved being in front of an audience and dreamed of getting paid to do it one day.

Her entry into the broadcasting industry was extremely challenging, but she refused to give up. Instead, she pushed through to become *"one of the wealthiest women in America and the highest paid entertainer in the world."*

🔥 BISHOP TD JAKES[39]

The prolific orator, Bishop TD Jakes, was known as *"the Bible Boy"* growing up. Although he was discouraged from preaching because of a speech impediment, he would practice preaching to an imaginary congregation. He would go on to work as the church music director and street evangelist.

In the 1980s, Bishop Jakes started a storefront church in West Virginia, while working full-time at the local chemical company. He frequently tells the story of how he and his family struggled financially in the beginning, but he didn't give up.

He pushed through, eventually launching the *Woman, Thou Art Loosed* phenomenon which opened the doors of opportunity for him. His church grew exponentially, and he is now one of the most recognized preachers and leaders in the world.

🔥 LISA NICHOLS[40]

Lisa Nichols is one of the world's most requested motivational speakers. As a young mother receiving public assistance, she struggled to make ends meet until the day she decided enough was enough.

As written in her media kit, *"in a moment of utter desperation, Lisa stood in front of her bathroom mirror...She imagined herself in front of thousands of people delivering a speech. She didn't leave out any detail. The laughter. The tears. The moments of deep connection. For the first time ever, Lisa discovered the Powerful Communicator in her. And today, Lisa has made it her mission to help others do the same."*

Her multi-million dollar enterprise includes six best-selling books, workshops/trainings, and programs that have transformed lives around the world.

🔥 GARY VAYNERCHUK[41]

Gary Vaynerchuk, Gary V. for short, also got started with humble beginnings. As a child, he lived with his family of eight in a studio apartment in Queens, NY. He began his entrepreneurial journey at the young age of seven with his lemonade franchise. Not only did he set up his own lemonade stand, but he convinced his friends to set up stands as well, and pay him a franchise fee.

Gary V. would then go on to help his father grow his liquor store from $4 million to $60 million in annual sales by adding an online component to the liquor store. In addition, he created his first episodic video show where he provided insights on wine tasting and pairing – increasing the visibility of his father's store, and ultimately sales.

From this initial show, doors of opportunity began to open for him, leading to a lucrative book deal and multiple business ventures. Today, Gary V. is recognized as one the of top entrepreneurial thought-leaders in the media and advertising space.

🔥 DAYMOND JOHN[42]

Daymond John's father left the family when he was ten years old, leaving his mom to struggle taking care of them. She would work multiple jobs to make ends meet, while inspiring him to be the best he could be.

While working at *Red Lobster*, Daymond saw a business opportunity to make and sell hats. His mom taught him how to sew and eventually mortgaged her home to invest in her son's dream. As a result, *FUBU* became an official business, production increased, and it became a household name, generating $350 million at its peak.

Daymond would then go on to become one of the original celebrity investors on *Shark Tank*, helping other entrepreneurs grow their businesses. In addition, he is the author of several best-selling books.

He's done the work, and his flame is fully lit.

ACKNOWLEDGMENTS

I want to thank God for allowing me to walk in my purpose and for extending Grace even when I don't deserve it.

To my wife, Victoria, you have been on this journey called life with me since we were 13 years old and have supported me through some crazy times.

To my children, Nia and Elzie (IV). You guys are my world and I hope that you know how much I love you. I'm so blessed to be your dad!

To my mother Snovia. You are my number one fan and are the reason I am able to stand here today as the man that I am. You pushed me when I needed to be pushed and believed in me when I didn't believe in myself.

To my siblings, Dr. Narcrisha Norman, Tiffany Reyes, Brian (Tasha) Flenard, ya'll are the best siblings I could have asked for and inspire me to be better every day. I'm so proud to be your brother and I hope I make you guys proud.

To Apostle Barnett. I watched you *"do life."* How you serve people, how you serve the Lord, and how you love your family. I would not be the man I am without the lessons you taught me and Victoria when we were under your leadership and even now from afar.

To Rev. Raynell Young, you are like a mother to me and I appreciate your support and prayers. My life is better because you're a part of it.

To my business family and supporters, I could not have done any of this without you. You inspire me and push me to be a better entrepreneur and human. You support my crazy ideas and hold me up when things get hard.

ABOUT THE AUTHOR

Don't pigeonhole Elzie D. Flenard III. Don't even try. Describe him this way, and he'll point out that one. Change your perspective, and he'll lead you down another path… maybe without you even realizing. He's a creative dude, an entrepreneur, a family man, a business owner. No *"box"* fits. It doesn't exist. He's a man of original thoughts, all products of unique thinking.

Above all, Elzie is a storyteller. He unpacks topics from unexpected directions, weaving myriad influences into his music, speaking and podcasting. Society, business, current events – you can never predict his take. Suffice to say, it's probably different than you've encountered. Why do things happen? How do they drive behavior? Most importantly, what do YOU think? Elzie wants to know. Dialog and conversation are great teachers. Listening inspires Elzie. Yes, listening. Almost a forgotten skill, in an era of endless chatter and oversize bullhorns.

See, everyone has a voice. Everyone has something to say. Via the power of podcasting, Elzie partners with businesses to turn their *"voice"* into a powerful marketing tool. Podcasting creates and cultivates relationships with consumers. A story about how a business began, about its products or services, or even its missteps, resonates through a human voice. Via *Podcast Town*, his podcasting company, Elzie helps businesses find their *"voice."* A voice doesn't have to be loud – just real. His clients repurpose their podcast content for blogs, or social media posts, or books. The ball rolls and rolls.

Elzie's foray into *Podcast Town* began not long after starting an Internet radio station. Its content tilted toward business, reflecting the founder's entrepreneurial bent. Even while working a decade in electrical engineering and electronics technology, Elzie had side gigs: a record label. A minor-league basketball team. A music production company. He's always been a tinkerer, going back to a childhood knack for taking things apart and putting them back together. Or writing his first song at age 5, a passion that continues today with multiple albums, EPs and singles under his belt. The holder of an MBA, and a B.S. in electronics systems technologies, you can always expect originality from Elzie. Just don't try to label him. No shoe fits...and he wouldn't wear it anyhow.

Launch, Grow, Maximize!

Your Podcast

We Take the "Hard" Out of Podcasting

For More Information, visit:

www.podcasttown.net

NOTES

INTRODUCTION
[1] "Honoring a Teacher: Christa McAuliffe's Lost Lessons," NASA, August 7, 2018, https://www.nasa.gov/feature/honoring-a-teacher-christa-mcauliffe-s-lost-lessons.
[2] *NBA*, "Kobe Bryant on the Mamba Mentality," YouTube video, https://www.youtube.com/watch?v=2EtHt6h_63o&t=33s.

CHAPTER ONE
[3] Brian Tracy quote from Brainy Quote website, https://www.brainyquote.com/quotes/brian_tracy_125679.
[4] Feelings Wheel, https://feelingswheel.com/.
[5] Linda and Charlie Bloom, "The Cost and Benefits of Emotional Honesty," Psychology Today, December 12, 2011, https://www.psychologytoday.com/us/blog/stronger-the-broken-places/201112/the-cost-and-benefits-emotional-honesty.

CHAPTER TWO
[6] Michael Jordan quote from Quotefancy website, https://quotefancy.com/quote/867513.
[7] Dr. Travis Bradberry & Dr. Jean Greaves, "Emotional Intelligence 2.0," Page 61, San Diego, CA: Talent SmartEQ, 2009.
[8] Tasha Eurich, "What Self-Awareness Really Is (and How to Cultivate It)," Harvard Business Review, January 04, 2018, https://hbr.org/2018/01/what-self-awareness-really-is-and-how-to-cultivate-it.
[9] "Benefits of Coaching," Institute of Coaching, https://instituteofcoaching.org/coaching-overview/coaching-benefits.

CHAPTER THREE
[10] Tony Robbins quote from Goodreads website, https://www.goodreads.com/quotes/877199.
[11] Form 10-K SEC Filings, U.S. Security and Exchange Commission, Fiscal Year Ended December 31, 1993. https://www.sec.gov/Archives/edgar/data/710979/0000950144-94-000803.txt.
[12] "CEA DVD Player Sales," The Digital Bits and Consume Electronic Association, page updated: 9/14/07 http://archive.thedigitalbits.com/articles/cemadvdsales.html.
[13] "The rise and fall of Blockbuster," Insider, August 20, 2020 https://www.businessinsider.com/rise-and-fall-of-blockbuster#despite-the-rise-of-netflix-and-redbox-blockbuster-was-at-its-peak-in-2004-10.
[14] BB Liquidating Inc. - 1:10-bk-14997, PacerMonitor, New York Southern Bankruptcy Court, Docket Item 1.0 - Filed: 09/23/2010,

http://www.pacermonitor.com/view/PXDYCPY/Blockbuster_Inc._nysbke-10-14997__0001.0.pdf.

CHAPTER FOUR

[15] Unknown author quote from Quotespedia, https://www.quotespedia.org/authors/u/unknown/forget-what-hurt-you-but-never-forget-what-it-taught-you-unknown/.

CHAPTER FIVE

[16] Winston Churchill quote from Goodreads website, https://www.goodreads.com/quotes/857718.

[17] Leo Buscaglia quote from Herioc website https://www.heroic.us/optimize/quotes/leo-buscaglia/its-not-enough-to-have-lived-we-should.

CHAPTER SIX

[18] Will Durant quote from Set Quotes website, https://www.setquotes.com/we-are-what-we-repeatedly-do-excellence-is-a-habit/.

[19] Aristotle quote from Goodreads website, https://www.goodreads.com/quotes/80461.

[20] Bruce Alberts, Alexander Johnson, Julian Lewis, Martin Raff, Keith Roberts, Peter Walter, Dennis Bray, and James D. Watson, "Molecular Biology of the Cell, 4th edition," National Library of Medicine, https://www.ncbi.nlm.nih.gov/books/NBK26843/.

CHAPTER EIGHT

[21] Brene Brown quote from Brainy Quote, https://www.brainyquote.com/quotes/brene_brown_553109.

CHAPTER NINE

[22] Muhammad Ali quote from Quotefancy, https://quotefancy.com/quote/869777/Muhammad-Ali-There-s-nothing-wrong-with-getting-knocked-down-as-long-as-you-get-right.

CHAPTER TEN

[23] Kobe Bryant quote from Quotefancy, https://quotefancy.com/quote/849284/Kobe-Bryant-Great-things-come-from-hard-work-and-perseverance-No-excuses.

[24] Marie Forleo, "Everything is Figureoutable," Page 66, New York: Portfolio/Penguin, 2019.

CHAPTER ELEVEN

[25] Emmitt Smith quote from Quotefancy website, https://quotefancy.com/quote/1418654/Emmitt-Smith-I-used-to-imagine-what-it-would-be-like-to-do-what-Jim-Brown-was-doing-I.

[26] Bible Gateway, https://www.biblegateway.com/passage/?search=Habakkuk%202%3A2&version=NKJV.

CHAPTER TWELVE
[27] Drake quote from Brainy Quote website, https://www.brainyquote.com/quotes/drake_551817?src=t_journey.
[28] Rizzarr, "Life Doesn't Happen to You, It Happens for You," Success, December 16, 2016, https://www.success.com/life-doesnt-happen-to-you-it-happens-for-you/.

CHAPTER THIRTEEN
[29] Iyanla Vanzant quote from Quotefancy website, https://quotefancy.com/quote/833591/Iyanla-Vanzant-Just-for-today-allow-yourself-to-embrace-all-that-you-are-every-moment.

CHAPTER FOURTEEN
[30] Bible Gateway, https://www.biblegateway.com/passage/?search=John%2013%3A34-35&version=ESV.
[31] Black Girls Code website, https://wearebgc.org/.
[32] Natasha Mascarenhas and Dominic-Madori Davis, "Black Girls Code Founder Kimberly Bryant has Been Fired by Her Board," Techcrunch, August 17, 2022, https://techcrunch.com/2022/08/17/black-girls-code-founder-kimberly-bryant-has-been-fired-by-her-board/.
[33] Ken Blanchard, Phil Hodges, and Phyllis Hendry, "Lead Like Jesus Revisited," Page 29, Nashville, TN: W Publishing, an imprint of Thomas Nelson, 2016.
Marie Forleo, "Everything is Figureoutable," Page 66, New York: Portfolio/Penguin, 2019.
[34] Ken Blanchard, Phil Hodges, and Phyllis Hendry, "Lead Like Jesus Revisited," Page 29, Nashville, TN: W Publishing, an imprint of Thomas Nelson, 2016.
Marie Forleo, "Everything is Figureoutable," Page 66, New York: Portfolio/Penguin, 2019.
[35] Bible Gateway, https://www.biblegateway.com/passage/?search=1+Corinthians+13&version=NLT. 1 Corinthians 13: 4-7, 13. BibleGateway.

CHAPTER FIFTEEN
[36] Lisa Nichols quote from Goodreads website, https://www.goodreads.com/work/quotes/44058572-abundance-now.
[37] "Michael Jordan Biography," Encyclopedia of World Biography, https://www.notablebiographies.com/Jo-Ki/Jordan-Michael.html.
[38] "Oprah Winfrey Biography," https://www.notablebiographies.com/We-Z/Winfrey-Oprah.html. Encyclopedia of World Biography.
[39] "Bishop T.D. Jake Biography," The History Makers, https://www.thehistorymakers.org/biography/bishop-td-jakes-33.

40 Motivating the Masses website, https://motivatingthemasses.com/about/lisa-nichols/.
41 Gary Vaynerchuk website, https://garyvaynerchuk.com/biography/.
42 Richard Feloni, "'Shark Tank' investor Daymond John explains how his mom helped FUBU become a $350 million company," Business Insider, https://businessinsider.com/shark-tanks-daymond-john-mother-2015-5.

www.ingramcontent.com/pod-product-compliance
Lightning Source LLC
Chambersburg PA
CBHW070952180426
43194CB00042B/2355